Published by
Free Your Mind Publishing
PO Box 70
Boston, MA 02131
(202) 251-7746
(202) 889-5056 (fax/orders)
orders@omekongo.com
http://www.freeyourmindpublishing.com

© 2011 by Omékongo Dibinga

Library of Congress Control Number: 2011940265

ISBN: 978-0-9760056-5-0-5

SAN: 2 5 6 - 1 8 8 3

Table of Contents

For my fellow UPstanders...

The *UP*standers Creed:

I cannot help others if I do not first help myself
I cannot upstand for others until I stand up for myself
I will give to myself until my cup runeth over
I will give to the world with all that's left over
I am a soldier for peace, a general for justice
Since giving is living, I know that I must give
By being a better me I can better society
So I will upstand for the world by being an upstander for me!

Introduction

It has been said that the two most important days in your life are the day you were born and the day you realize *why* you were born. Congratulations! You just scored a 50% on life's two-question exam. But we're taught that 50% isn't good enough right? Nothing short of 100% right? If you chose to open this book, you probably are experiencing some form of anxiety in your life like:

"What class should I register for?"

"Did I choose the right school?"

"Did I pick the right major?"

"Where am I going to find a summer internship?"

"Does this professor believe in the 15-minute rule?"

"When will I hear about my financial aid package?"

"Will she accept me as a friend on Facebook?"

"I'm about to graduate and I haven't found a job! WTF?"

"Will I even be able to get a job in this economy?"

"What's this drink really composed of?"

"Um...it's been 5 minutes. WHY hasn't she accepted my Facebook friend request?!"

OMG! If you're anything like me, these serious questions are probably being asked in addition to the other pressing questions in your life like:

"How do I stop genocide in Darfur?"

"How can I make my campus less homophobic?"

"What can I do to end sex slavery across the globe?"

"Why am I the only one who seems to care that there are homeless people in the richest country on earth?"

"How long can we continue depleting nature's resources and act like it's OK?"

"When will we learn that adolescent domestic abuse is real?"

"What's happening with our wildlife population?"

"How many Congolese had to die so I can have a discount on my cell phone?"

And if you're *really* like me, you've thought about all of this *before* you made it to breakfast!

It's no wonder that across this country and abroad, college students are stressed out. Every single moment you feel like you are faced with a decision that can alter your life or the lives of others. Furthermore, you have learned the age-old truth that your indecision is actually a decision so you know that even your silence has consequences somewhere, somehow, and at any time. You are so focused on the *next* thing (from the next class to the next war) that you've literally lost the ability to live in the now. As I've traveled across this country speaking to upstanders like you on the importance of raising awareness and ending conflict in the Congo, the Sudan, Burma, and other places, I have encountered countless other students like you who are so caught up in the daily grind of college life that they have not taken the time to take care of themselves. How can I see the signs? I can see the signs because I was just like you.

Picture it. Georgetown University. It's the fall semester of 1996. As a Congolese-American, fighting for justice and peace in the Congo has been the family business. For literally hundreds of years, my family has been fighting for peace back home. So imagine the helplessness I felt on the way to class when I learned that war erupted there. Class was a blur. All I could think about was calling my parents to see what I could do to stop the war. This did not make for a smooth transition into a school I just transferred into from Morehouse College, but that wasn't all I was consumed with that year.

During that one year at Georgetown before I went to study abroad in Senegal, I was a Student Activities Commissioner (where I represented 9 student groups from the Ballroom Dancing Club, The Irish Club, and Circolo Italiano to The Hmong Society, The Native American Club and South Vietnamese Society), member of the African Student Group, NAACP, Black Student Alliance, co-created a group called Brother-to-Brother, and found myself spending time at Howard University protesting whatever it was that led students there to have a sit-in in the administration building. These are just the activities that I remember! Not to mention the fact that transitioning from a freshman to a sophomore and picking a major in a new school meant going from writing 7 papers my freshman year to 42 during my sophomore year. Oh joy. Oh *freakin'* joy!

Actually, despite all of that, there was actually a lot of freakin' joy—*eventually*. Why? See in addition to all of these activities, I was also part of the intramural basketball team. I also found a place to practice martial arts at night. I love martial arts. I also found time to do other activities like roller blade, workout in the gym, and of course perform my poetry at the open mics! Oh yeah, did I mention that my high school sweetheart also happened to be a student at Georgetown? Trust me though; I transferred to Georgetown for its great reputation in international affairs (That's my story and I'm sticking to it)! What I was able to do during that hectic year is find balance and that's what this book is all about—finding college-life balance while changing the world at the same time.

I don't know you, but if you opened this book and you are still reading up to this point, it's because you are a difference maker. You are an upstander. There is no complicated definition for an upstander. You simply see a problem, and you realize that silence is compliance and so you decide to stand up for what you believe in. You want to change something in this world for the better whether it's beautification of a street in your neighborhood or ending genocide. Come to think of it, if you're still reading this, I *do* know you. You've sacrificed yourself to make others happy. You've given of your own free time because you feel that you are so privileged to be where you are that you should do something to help those less fortunate. If you ever find time to go to parties, you find it hard to fully enjoy yourself because you're thinking about your cause. I know you all too well for I am you and you are me.

The goal of this book is to show you how to have a balanced life while still carving out your life as it relates to your academic and professional careers, and your social justice cause. The goal of this book is to show you that it's ok to be committed to a cause, but you must first be committed to yourself. Consider this book your guide to living the same life you are living right now, but stress free. It *is* possible to have the career of your dreams and be happy. It *is* possible for you to end an issue such as sex slavery or environmental degradation and still have a life—no—a *happy* life. This is the book I needed to read *before* I went to college (actually, before I went to high school). The life lessons I learned from my undergraduate to the doctoral level in education are poured into this book. If you don't believe me, upstander, sit down (for once) and just read on.

Chapter 1: *You* are your only competition!

"I'm running a one-person race."

-Oprah Winfrey

"I looked in the mirror...my only opponent."

-Jay-Z

GPAs. Class rankings. School rankings. Face it. You've been pitted against your academic peers from the day you stepped into pre-k, but you don't really start to pay attention until you get into high school. This is indeed a capitalist society and so competition is encouraged but in the world of academia, competition is encouraged to a fault. You're reminded every day through emails, school bulletins, and of course social media, on who aced a state exam, who received a perfect score on her SAT, etc., etc. The only pressure that can rival what is seen at school is the pressure you may receive at home from well-intentioned (and not so well-intentioned) parents and other loved ones:

"Be like your [*insert name of relative who is the white sheep of the family*]!"

"You need to become a [*insert name of career that holds prestige but may end up holding more of your bank account balance as you repay loans forever*]!"

"You're never gonna get married with that attitude!"

"You don't wanna end up like [*insert relative who everyone thinks is a failure but probably failed because he took the advice above at the expense of his dreams*]!"

"You have to get a college degree if you want a chance to succeed!"

"You can't just [*insert name of the activity that you feel the most liberty partaking in and you would choose as a profession if we lived in a world that didn't need money*] all day. You need to get a real job!"

With these types of pressures bearing down on you daily, it can be very difficult to think that you were put on this earth to pursue *your* chosen purpose in life and not someone else's. You feel that since someone else is paying your tuition, you owe it to him or her to pursue what *he or she* wanted. Or because your parent or guardian wasn't successful in his or her career, you feel you have to right the ship and let them live vicariously through you. You just feel like you are in debt to someone or something at every step of your journey. Here's what you have to realize though: to continue on with this mentality is not traveling on *your* journey. You're traveling on *their* journey. This will be explored more in a later chapter. Let's first look at how we can deal with accepting the fact that we deserve to even be in school in the first place.

Listen upstander. I'll make this as clear as possible. Slavery in America legally ended a long time ago (though of course there are issues such as human trafficking that we are working to end in this day age). You cannot allow yourself to be a slave to someone else's dream—period. You survived a battle against millions of sperm so that you can achieve your greatness and the only way you are going to achieve that greatness is by realizing that you are here to choose your own path in life. I know you may be thinking: "This sounds great Omekongo but how do I achieve this in my own life now?" Let me show you how.

What you have to remember is that no one has walked in your shoes so they are not competing with you. Zig Ziglar once said that we have to remember to not tear ourselves down as we build other people up. When I was at Morehouse and Georgetown, I was amazed by all of the stories I read about my

12

fellow classmates. John was valedictorian at the best private school in the country. Jamil was captain of the debate team for 2 years and his team never lost. Jasmine started an organization to help battered women at age 12 and at 19 has helped more than 75 women get back on their feet and live independently. Abdul since the age of 15 has been working on ending the Arab-Israeli conflict. Lastly, I was literally taking classes with people who were the children of senators, ambassadors, and corporate tycoons. The first thing you may be telling yourself, like I did is: "I don't deserve to be here. I can't compete with these guys."

What I had to do was take a step back. Another stigma I had going against me was that, as an African American at a top school like Georgetown, many people instantly thought that I was only there because of affirmative action. No one cared about my 3.74 GPA coming out of Morehouse or that I graduated from the oldest high school in the country, Boston Latin School (founded in 1635), as a member of the National Honor Society. You have to realize that people will see you and what they don't already know about you, they will make up. You may have experienced similar stigmas because of your gender, sexual orientation, race, culture, religion, or even the region of the country you come from. You can't do anything about what they think so stop trying to prove that you belong. You have to just be.

You have to realize that once the admissions committee sent you that acceptance letter, you were placed on an equal footing with all of your classmates. You belong there just as much as they do. Yes, there are some who may have come in with higher skill sets, but that's what tutoring and other forms of academic assistance are for. You have to accept the fact that something *you* wrote in your essay for school or something about *your* academic background made you worthy and that's *all* you need to know. If you were not fit for your school, you simply would not have been accepted.

What you also have to realize is that you are the product of serious experiences that the average person probably could not have survived. What I quickly learned in school, and what I often tell students with whom I speak is that you have been through some experiences that would have led many other people to take their own lives. There were so many students I saw who came from backgrounds so privileged that they literally didn't have a care in the world. I am not saying that all privileged students don't have challenges. That's obviously not true. What I am saying is that there were some who have had a relatively easy life and some crumbled under simple academic pressures and dropped out by midterms of their first semester even though they were on full scholarships. Some simply couldn't handle the responsibility of being away from home. Some got caught up in the party life. Some felt there was no point in studying because their parents will always take care of them.

I found myself thinking that if I could *survive* growing up in the Roxbury, Massachusetts at the height of the crack epidemic where gang violence was rampant, I can *thrive* in school. If I can *survive* living in an era where young black males walked around with shirts saying "Black men: endangered species" because of the rate at which we were being murdered or incarcerated, I could *thrive* in school. If I can *survive* the racism I experienced (like white students wearing white hoods to school on the day it was time to vote for high school class president and I was a candidate), I can *thrive* in college. Lastly, if I can *survive* the verbal and physical abuse I suffered at the hands of my class(less)mates because I had a foreign name and wore hand-me-downs because of our financial challenges, I can *thrive* in school. These experiences taught me that I am in competition with no one but myself because no one has walked in my shoes.

So what have you survived that should make studying and writing some papers a snap for you? Did you make it to college despite growing up poor? Did you make it despite experiencing racism, anti-Semitism, and homophobia? Did you emerge from the anti-immigrant sentiment and Islamophobia sweeping America? Did you survive domestic or sexual abuse? Did you survive growing up in a household where drug or alcohol abuse was rampant? Did you survive political persecution in your homeland? Whatever it is upstander, get this in your head: you survived. Now it 's time to *thrive*! I don't think most people could have survived the challenges I dealt with growing up. Quite frankly, however, I don't know if I could have survived some of the challenges that *you* have dealt with growing up that I have learned about while traveling the globe. What I have learned is that the words Les Brown said ring true for us every day: you have been picked out to be picked on!

Life is a test (pun intended). As Willie Jolley said: the difference between school and life is that in school, you get the test after you receive the lessons. In life however, you get the tests *before* you receive the lessons. You are tried and tested. You have survived. Because of that, you have to right now stop comparing yourselves to other people. You are here for a reason. You may even know people who have lost their lives to similar pressures but you're still here. Use that as a reason to hold your head with pride, not down in despair.

Activity: What challenges have I survived in life and how?

1. _____

_____

_____

2. _____

_____

_____

3. _____

_____

_____

4. _____

_____

_____

5. _____

_____

_____

Get more paper if you need it. The point here is to use this activity to realize that if you can get through what you have written above, school should be relatively easy. You can't develop success amnesia. Don't forget what you did to get through prior challenging experiences. Develop success transference and apply the same skills to the challenge of school.

Chapter 2: Follow what *you* feel

"We're all born as originals but most of us die as copies."

-Les Brown

*"Your career is what you're paid for. Your calling is what you're **made** for."*

- Zig Ziglar

As I said earlier, you have to realize that you have been picked out to be picked on. You survived the battle against millions of sperm and made it to earth. As Oprah Winfrey said, you were validated because you were born—period. As simple as it sounds, you and I know that it's not *that* simple in practice because we live in a society where we are constantly reminded that who we are is not good enough.

When Michael Jordan was at the height of his basketball fame, there was a huge campaign in the media to be "like Mike." Here are the words to the song:

Sometimes I dream
That he is me
You've got to see that's how I dream to be
I dream I move, I dream I groove
Like Mike
If I could Be Like Mike
Like Mike
Oh, if I could Be Like Mike
Be Like Mike, Be Like Mike
Again I try
Just need to fly
For just one day if I could
Be that way
I dream I move
I dream I groove
Like Mike
If I could Be Like Mike
I wanna be, I wanna be
Like Mike
Oh, if I could Be Like Mike

I mean goodness gracious! How can you feel comfortable in your own skin when songs like these are telling you to be more like your idol? But that's the purpose of advertising right? Not to make you love yourself but to hate the fact that you don't act, sing, dance, or look like someone else. This song could be about Taylor Swift, Drake, Damien Rice, Rihanna, Carrie Underwood, Angelina Jolie, or anyone else. We are simply told on a daily basis that we are not good enough in our own skin. But if it was just the media committing this crime, maybe we would be OK dealing with it because we could just turn off the TV but again, it's not that easy.

In school we are also taught that who we are is not good enough. Just watch any video by the great educator Sir Ken Robinson and others who deal in the field of culturally relevant teaching and teaching about creativity. School sucks out our creativity like blood to a vampire and focuses on manufacturing students who will sit still and take orders. Sir Ken Robinson recounts a story of a woman in the 1930s before Attention Deficit Disorder (ADD) was "invented" as he says. This woman was having a problem with her daughter. The child just couldn't sit still and the school thought she had a learning disorder. She took her daughter to a specialist who conducted an experiment where the child was left in a room by herself with the radio playing.

At the end of the experiment, after watching the child, the doctor concluded that the child wasn't sick. She was a dancer. Instead of placing this child in some form of institution or medicating her, the mother enrolled her in a dance school. The child's name was Gillian Lynne and she went on to be the choreographer of two of the world's best theatrical pieces, *CATS* and *Phantom of the Opera*. If she were alive today, Sir Ken Robinson says she would be medicated and told to sit down. He says that we are educating people out of their creative capacities. This is how our education system has operated over the years and it is no different today. The same problem is happening to you right now.

How many times have you been told that your work in school isn't right because you did not incorporate the ideas of Shakespeare, Kant, Dr. King, Weber, Albright, or someone else? I know that even up to the doctoral level, I have found myself thinking that I am sometimes regurgitating the ideas of others. Too many times I have felt like I was just in class to reproduce the ideas of others. Instead of being "like Mike" it was be like Professor Johnson. This can be frustrating for upstanders like us whose minds are constantly thinking about changing the world or our community but there *is* a way out.

The most important tool you must develop when dealing with the aforementioned issues is the philosophy that "I am still finding my way." You have to realize that your classes, jobs, internships, etc. are nothing more than learning experiences that will help you figure it out. Someone once said that there are no failures in life, only lessons. Of course we've all heard the saying that when you lose in life, don't lose the lesson. While it's important while you're in school to learn what it is that you want to do with your life, it is equally important to learn what you ***don't*** want to do with your life. You have to chew the meat and spit out the bones. If you choose to continue your academic career, you have to understand that the classes and other activities that don't fulfill you are not the end of the world but part of the process.

So how do you know the difference between following what you feel and feeling like you're just a follower? It all comes down to the classes and activities that you love the most. If you were told that you need to be an economics major at your liberal arts school but you really loved that psychology class you took in your spring semester, then sign up for more psychology classes! If you came in looking to be an English major but really developed a love for drama, then take some drama classes! Now you may be asking: "What about the people who really want me to be a [inserting yet again the name of a career that someone else may have chosen because they are living vicariously through you]?" My answer? Forget them.

Look. I am the child of immigrants from the Congo. Like many children of immigrants (and I think it's the same for children of non-immigrants too), I felt the pressure to choose a particular path because this was part of why most immigrants come to America in the first place: in pursuit of a dream and better educational opportunities. All of my siblings experienced it in some way, shape, or form. One was supposed to be the doctor, the other a lawyer, etc. Today, however, none of my 8 siblings and I are doing the careers that my father probably wanted us to do. Though I'm sure my father may have had some disappointment in that, what I know for sure (because he told me) is that if he were to die today, he would die a happy man because his children represent the spirit of what he wanted us to be in America and the same is true for my mother.

At the end of the day, my parents wanted their children to be compassionate for humanity, never forget where they came from, and give back to their community and that's what we are all doing in our own particular ways and professions. What you have to realize is that at the end of the day, the people you feel will condemn you for doing what you love will come around, as long as in your heart you are a good person. This is true in comparatively small issues like choosing a career but it is also true for people who aspire to change the world for the better.

Just think about it. Many of the people we honor today were condemned for standing up for what they believed in. Dr. King was assassinated for his beliefs and now there is a national memorial to his legacy. Nelson Mandela spent 27 years in jail for his beliefs but then became the President of South Africa. The list goes on and on from Muhammad Ali to Jay-Z, who was condemned through much of his career for violent and misogynistic lyrics and is now putting on benefit concerts for victims of the horrendous 911 attacks. At the end of the day, you will be respected by those you fear will reject you so stop worrying about their approval and do what *you* feel. That's what you are here to do! Your vision was given to you and only you so once you make it a reality, the world will open its doors to you.

Finally on this point, I must share my own story on choosing my career path that led me to writing this book in the first place. As a graduate student at The Fletcher School of Law & Diplomacy, one of the top graduate international affairs programs in the world, I was intent on studying for the Foreign Service Exam. My dream was to be the American Ambassador to Congo. During my first semester, however, the 911 attacks happened. While I understood the United States' response, I did not agree with the way the response was executed.

One day during the spring semester, a diplomat came to school to talk to us about being in the Foreign Service. The response he gave me to the question I asked him changed the direction of my life forever. I asked him what does someone in the Foreign Service do when he is part of the government but disagrees with a government policy? The diplomat said that a member of the Foreign Service does not have to verbally and publicly endorse a policy of the government, but that person also cannot speak out *against* the policy either. I stopped studying for the exam that day and never took it.

What the diplomat said made perfect sense of course and so this is not a knock against the Foreign Service. No organization wants public insubordination and would like to handle conflicts behind closed doors. What I told myself that day, however, is that life is too short for *me* to worry about someone telling me what I can't say. I have too much on my mind and need to be a free thinker. I'm sure that decision disappointed some members of my family, some friends, as well as academic advisors but you and I probably never would have met had I not made that decision. Since then, I committed myself to spreading a message of peace and hope through my own means: through motivational speaking, hip-hop, and spoken word poetry. That decision has led me to almost 20 countries, and television and radio appearances in over 150 countries. Most importantly, it has led me to meet great people like you who are on the same journey that I am and use my life as a lesson and inspiration to others.

Though I could not really see what was to be back then, I stepped out on faith, trusted myself, and made a decision that I thought was best for *me*. If it worked for me, it can work for you. If you were in that same predicament, you may have chosen to still take the exam because you believe in working on the inside to make change and that's fine too! As long as your intentions are in the right place, do what *you* feel! Don't be "like Mike." Be the first you!

Activity: write down everything you were told to be when you "grow up."

1. _____
2. _____
3. _____
4. _____
5. _____

Now write down all the things you actually told *yourself* you want to be in life (you don't have to fill out all 5, especially if you've only had one or two dreams that you've wanted to achieve in life).

1. _____
2. _____
3. _____
4. _____
5. _____

If lists one and two seem to be polar opposites, you must go back and reread this chapter and start working on doing whatever it takes to make your second list the first and only list!

Lastly, it is important to quote the immortal Steve Jobs, founder of Apple. In his commencement speech at Stanford in 2005, Jobs said the following words to the audience, which represent the essence of this chapter. Read on and heed his advice:

> *Your time is limited, so don't waste it living someone else's life. Don't be trapped by dogma — which is living with the results of other people's thinking. Don't let the noise of others' opinions drown out your own inner voice. And most important, have the courage to follow your heart and intuition. They somehow already know what you truly want to become. Everything else is secondary.*

Chapter 3: Find your release

So now you are starting to get an idea of what it takes to start to live life on your terms. This may be hard to do because for most of your life you have been living on someone else's terms and now you are getting a taste of independence. In this process, two extremes tend to happen: either you become so nervous with your newfound independence that you stay in a bubble and take no chances with anything new or you vow to have every experience that you've never had at home. True success at the collegiate level comes in the middle of that.

I had the opportunity to speak to two Division I NCAA football teams in New York and Maryland. I was speaking about the importance of striving for greatness and understanding the responsibility that comes with being a popular athlete. In both presentations, I heard a statement from some students that sounded something like this:

> *I feel like I can't even think for myself on this campus because every minute of the day is planned for us. From the time we have to wake up to practice time, study hours, gym hours, and more. How am I supposed to be a free thinker like you say and develop myself when every minute of the day has to be devoted to something or someone else?*

Before I even attempt to answer that question, let me state the obvious: it's not only athletes that feel this way. You feel the same way too. Between classes, activities, internships, and jobs, you feel that every second of the day is programmed. Whenever you *do* have a break, you find yourself either studying or finding some other way to work on your social justice cause. On the rare time that you actually do take some form of break in the form of a party or going to the gym, you *still* find yourself thinking about your cause or your academic and professional life. If you also have financial difficulties in school, it becomes almost impossible to focus on anything. So what do you do?

The first thing you have to remember is the first few lines of the "UPstander's Creed" from the beginning of this book:

> *"I cannot help others if I do not first help myself*
> *I cannot upstand for others until I stand up for myself"*

You must understand that you are no good to any movement, class, job, etc. unless **you** make **you** the top priority. Does that mean that you say "screw the world" because what you want is the only thing that matters? No, what it means is that you have to make sure your mind, body, and spirit are in the right place before you jump into any endeavor.

For example, before I do any performance, I take time to interact with the crowd beforehand, but a few minutes before the show, I have to remove myself from everyone in the room. I go into a corner or even to a quiet place outside. I don't practice my performance pieces. I listen to several songs that help get me in the mood like John Lennon's "Imagine" or Michael Jackson's "Earth Song" because they remind me of what I am doing my work for. Honestly though, if I need to get amped up for a very high energy show, I watch all of the Joker scenes from "The Dark Knight" or Michael Jackson's live performance of "Billie Jean" from his 1992 concert in Bucharest. Before I perform, I simply have to take time to listen to a great performance or watch one. This gets me in the proper zone to go out and give as great a performance as I can possibly give that day.

If I don't take the time to mentally prepare myself to give my best performance, I simply won't give the best performance possible. If I spent time talking to everyone, writing text messages, or answering phone calls before my performance starts, by the time I got on stage I would pretty much be asking the audience: "What am I supposed to be doing here again?" I see it all the time from other performers who just walk on stage with no regard for the audience. They'll speak in to the microphone chewing gum and say things out loud like: "Which piece should I do next? Hmmm…. Nah, not that one. Maybe this one." This has led them to forget lines and just not connect with the audience on several levels.

This is what I do for my performances and you must do the same because life is just an act at the end of the day. You have to prepare yourself for the role of a lifetime—playing yourself! Do what you need to do to make sure you're in spiritual alignment with yourself and you do that by finding your release. What's a release? A release is the activity that you engage in that when you do it, you feel completely at peace. This is the activity that, if we lived in a world where we didn't need money, you would do this activity all day. For LeBron James it would be playing basketball or singing for Shania Twain. It probably would have been helping more children across the globe for the late Mother Teresa (who did her work without a desire for money). For you it might be reading non-academic works, playing a sport, taking yoga, singing, volunteering at a community center, etc. Without this activity, you simply just don't feel complete, yet it amazes me how many incomplete students I see walking around on campuses from at least middle school up to the doctoral level.

I once spoke at the national IMPACT conference on service. Afterwards, a student came up to me asking about the quotation I shared (also at the beginning of this book) about the most important days in your life being the day you were born and the day you realize *why* you were born. She was asking me about the latter part of that quotation because she hadn't found herself and figured out why she was here on earth. We started talking about things she liked to do and one of the things she said she enjoyed was practicing yoga. I told her that was great and asked her when the last time she did it was. She told me two semesters ago!

How can you find peace in the world if you remove the activities from your life that you feel are integral to your development? At the MA and PhD level, I constantly ran into students who told me they used to be a dancer or some other form of artist before they entered the program and they miss it so much. I always found myself asking: why do you have to lose it? My belief is that when you separate yourself from what you love, everything else suffers. Once I entered my doctoral program, I found myself a bit lost because the topics I thought I should study just didn't vibe with me. Once I changed my focus to art and social change, I was like a new person! Even my professors told me that my papers were much more poignant when I was writing about what I actually loved. Even at Fletcher, I was using poetry as a way to process what I learned in the classroom and these weren't art classes. I'm talking about classes like "Law & Development" and "Political Economy of Development." I can't remember any other students doing the same. I must have really looked like a weirdo in class but hey, it was fun!

So you have to have fun at the end of the day. Make time to do what *you* love. It's not your schedule that is preventing you from doing what you love. It's the misplaced belief that you have to separate yourself from what it is that you love that led you to not even consider putting what you love to do on your "To do list" in the first place. Take a chance on yourself. Factor in YOU in your daily schedule. Find that time during the day that no one can take from you whether it's 5 minutes to meditate or 45 minutes for a game of squash. Do it. Do it now. You won't regret it. It might actually save your collegial life!

Activity: write down the 5 activities you would do more if we lived in a world where we did not need money.

1. _____
2. _____
3. _____

4. _____

5. _____

Now answer the following question: given that many of these activities are offered at or around your school, why are you not doing one or ***all*** of them?

_____

_____

_____

Now ask yourself honestly: are the excuses you just provided really enough to make you stop doing what you claim you love to do? I don't think so. Nothing is worth giving up what you love. Get to living. Get to loving. Live to do what you love. The rapper Drake said that everybody dies but not everybody lives. Don't get so caught up in the supposed mandatory rigors of the day that you forget to do what you love. When Dr. King was assassinated at the age of 39, it was when they cut him open for the autopsy that they realized he had the heart of a 60-year old. This was due to the stress of the movement. Don't let a movement kill you. Give life to yourself so you can give more life to the movement. Find your release and never let it go!

Chapter 4: Seek out mentors

Rapper Kanye West is notorious for celebrating ignorance. Despite the fact that he is the child of educated parents, he proudly stated on one of his albums that he doesn't read. Several years ago he also had a song called "You can't tell me nothin'." Though people listen to these words and laugh or think he's being clever, they are complete and utter lies. Kanye West is a creative genius lyrically as well as on the production side, but he is also the product of great mentorship. He rose to international prominence under the tutelage of Jay-Z and actually has spoken in several songs about his burning desire to just get Jay-Z a beat because he knew he would be set from there. The rest is history.

In this day and age of "i" everything (iPhone, iTunes, etc.), it saddens me to see how many of your peers are so consumed with themselves to the point that they have not thought about the importance of mentorship. Let me be clear. This is not just the case with your generation. At all ages, we are all consumed in a "me" and more specifically, a "gimme" society. If you really want to take yourself to the next level, you have to find good mentors. You have to seek people out people who are going to aid you in your personal, professional, and academic development. Remember, just as there is no "i" in team; there is no "i" in "upstander." You don't have to do this all by yourself!

If you want to really start finding mentors, you have to switch your mentality. In college, we tend to develop a mentality that everyone is against us if we don't get the right grade, get denied for a job, taken off a waiting list for a class, etc. This kind of thinking will make you become very insular and the more insular you become, the more opportunities you will lose out on. There are many ways on the college and high school level that you can develop good mentors because, quite honestly, there are still mentors from high school that I am still in contact with to this day. So let's talk about some concrete ways that you can begin to find some good mentors while still in school because these people can help you throughout your entire career in the form of recommendations, job opportunities and more.

Before you even start your freshmen year, you should start getting an idea of the names of the professors that you are going to have. Even if you are not sure which professor you will have, contact all of them. For example, if you know you have to take "Law & Order 101" and you know that there are 3 professors who will teach that class, email all three of them separately and introduce yourself. Let them know where you're from and what your interests are and that you are excited to take their class. On the first day of school, go up to the professor and introduce yourself and remind them that you were the person who emailed her. Also, make it a point to see the professor after doing the first set of readings and ask questions!

This may sound corny, but the effect of this is that your professor will know you before she gets to know others and this will help you. I have been teaching for a very long time and I'll be very honest, relationships count. Everybody can't get an A. If there is a class where every student gets an A, unless the professor is someone like Bill Clinton, the professor will most likely not keep his job. Someone *has* to get an A, B, C, D, or F. If a professor has two students to choose between giving one an A- and another student a B+, the professor will choose the student with whom she has the best relationship to get the higher grade. It's just a fact.

In hindsight, I can recall several situations where I believe that I would have received a higher grade if I simply had a better relationship with my teachers and professors. In the activist mindset that I possessed in some of my classes, I constantly took positions that challenged some of my professors and didn't develop good relationships with them. What's interesting is that there were teachers that I completely butted heads with but I still received an A because I was respectful but I *also* had a good relationship with them.

Conversely, there were several relationships that I didn't develop with professors because of personality conflicts and even though I knew I was performing academically at a higher level of some of my peers (based on seeing their work with my own eyes), this affected my grade.

As a teaching assistant at Georgetown to Dr. Michael Eric Dyson, I had a student come up to me after class just to talk about absolutely nothing for a good five minutes. The end result though is that I know his name out of a class of over 100 students. I'm sure he knew exactly what he was doing when he introduced himself to me! Get to know your professors people!

As a student organizer, there are other ways that you can develop relationships and find good mentors. Most if not all school organizations must have some form of sponsor. This is someone that you don't have to just work with for a semester or two. Actively speak with them about opportunities in your field. Also find people who work with various organizations in and outside of your school community. There are so many hardworking adults out there who would just be delighted that you've simply taken an interest in their work that they'll tell you everything they know!

Lastly, don't forget that fellow students can also serve as mentors. Find students who have taken the classes you have taken or who have worked at the same places where you would like to work or intern. Don't just read feedback surveys online. Talk to them. Whether we are living in tough economic times or times of great prosperity, many people get jobs more so because of their social networks than their actual résumé. The more genuine relationships you develop, the better your chances are down the road as you advance professionally. Also remember, that if you are in a position to be a mentor, decide to be the mentor you wish you had when you were at your potential mentee's station in life! As Dr. Maya Angelou said, as soon as you receive, give. As soon as you learn, teach. Remember that yes, you are always going to be a student in the class of life, but life gets a little easier to understand and navigate when you take advantage of true, quality mentorship. It's not just about the difference between an A or a B. it's about having quality people by your side who will help you realize that you don't have to go it alone.

Activity: Write the names of 5 people (students, professors, etc.) who can serve as potential mentors and what they could mentor you on. Write them today! Whether it's to meet for lunch, visit during office hours, do it now!

1. _____
   _____

2. _____
   _____

3. _____
   _____

4. _____
   _____

5. _____
   _____

Chapter 5: "Seek to understand before you seek to be understood."

This quotation comes from Stephen Covey's classic book, *The Seven Habits of Highly Effective People*. There are several ways to dissect this quote but for you, there is one particularly important topic that this quotation is very relevant for: student group envy! Yes, it exists. Let's just put it out there. There are student groups, even groups that may represent the same cause, that hate each other. There could be personality issues, jealousy over who got more funding, and more. You would think that this may have nothing to do with achieving a successful life balance as a student but you would be very wrong.

The fact of the matter is that one of the reasons that we are often frustrated on college campuses with the work that we do is because we feel as if no one understands us. We don't understand how people could just not give a damn about the rainforests, global warming, the direction of American politics, education, poverty, genocide, *Jersey Shore*, *Real Housewives*, *Top Chef*, *Basketball Wives*, and more. It sucks that I'm putting Snooki in the same conversation as genocide but yes; people can find ways to not like each other for very small reasons. As I said in the chapter on mentorship, however, we have to change our mentality because that's what we have instant control over.

Rather than being angry that people aren't supporting your cause, ask yourself whose cause are **you** supporting? One of the greatest experiences I had as an undergraduate was serving as a Student Activities Commissioner. As I stated earlier, I represented 9 multicultural and artistic student groups from the South Vietnamese Society to Ballroom Dancing. Without that experience, most of my work on campus probably would have surrounded organizations that dealt with black causes like the Black Student Alliance or the African Student Group. When I had to sit down and listen to the experiences and needs of these other organizations, my college life changed for the better for two reasons, which can also help you in your campus outreach.

The first benefit of working with these groups is that I was forced to see issues from a different perspective. I may not have agreed with the politics or philosophies of some of these organizations, but I respected their rights as a campus group to organize for their cause and fought on their behalf. In order to do that, I had to actually go to the events these groups put on and see what they were all about. It was truly an eye-opening experience. At the end of the school year, one student from the Hmong Society (the Hmong are an Asian ethnic group) gave me a wooden turtle, which has great significance in their culture. They would not have given me this if they did not feel that I represented their interests. I showed that, to the best of my ability, I understood them. I also did this for other groups and individuals that I came across on Georgetown's very international campus, which led to the second benefit.

The second benefit was that people who did not ordinarily get involved in black causes began coming to events that I was involved in. They were more willing to ask questions and listen to perspectives on issues facing the black community that they may not have, had they not encountered me in their settings (or other black leaders who supported their causes). When people feel that you understand them or at least made an attempt to, they are more likely to understand, or attempt to understand you.

So ask yourself, are you genuinely interested in supporting other organizations or at least going to their meetings to hear them out? Are you sending delegates from your group to other rallies and info sessions? What attempts have you earnestly made to hear what other people have to say? The more you spend your time listening to others, the more time people will spend listening to you. It's really that simple. If people see you as someone who is only self-absorbed in your own cause, they will never want to work with you. You have to face it: your cause is not the most pressing cause in the world for everyone. For me, the genocide that has been taking place in the Congo for over a decade is the most important issue for me to work on ending. Just because this is important to me does not mean that it is more important than you trying to feed the homeless. We all have our causes that are important to us. Our job is not to shut down someone else for being committed to another cause. Our job is to seek to understand each other so we can advance our goals as a human collective.

Don't be arrogant in believing that only your cause matters. That will consume you in a way that will be detrimental to your health as well as your reputation. Part of achieving college-life balance is realizing that there is not one small pie of finite resources. Working together allows us to make a bigger pie and work together on causes that may be more related than we think. If you want people to understand you, you simply have to understand them. There is no way of getting around that.

Activity: Whom will you seek to understand?
In your attempt to be a better part of your campus community, write down the names of five organizations that you will seek to network with by attending meetings, rallies, or social events. Also write down why you picked these organizations. Don't just do it just to say you did it. Do this in the same spirit that you would want someone to have if they were going to come to your meeting.

1. _____
2. _____
3. _____
4. _____
5. _____

Chapter 6: Know that you will win...eventually

So why is it that we get involved in a movement in the first place? It's because we want to make change. We want to make a difference in life. We want to impact our community from the smallest to the largest ways possible. On a daily basis, we obsess over how exactly we are going to make change. One of the biggest battles we face, however, is time. We get frustrated that change is not happening fast enough. In terms of issues such as genocide, we obsess over the fact that at every second, some baby, some grandfather, some mother is being murdered. In terms of the environment, you may feel like every time you see a car go by, the ozone layer is becoming weaker and weaker. How in the world do we deal with this? You have to develop patience and believe in your heart that you will win...eventually. How do I know this to be true? History is my witness.

Think about the genocides and other forms of mass killings that have taken place throughout the world. The victims have outlasted the perpetrators. Native Americans are still here. Armenians are still here. African Americans, Jews, Tutsis, Congolese, and more are *all* still here. Some of these groups such as Native Americans and African Americans survived literally centuries of murder, slavery, and injustice and they're still here. Evil cannot outlast good. Perpetrators of genocide and mass atrocities like Hitler and Saddam Hussein end up hiding out in ditches or taking their own life while the survivors move on. You will win.

I can cite example after example of progress that other social movements have made such as the movement to end sweatshop labor and conflict diamonds or movements to create fair trade coffee and end sex trafficking. Now let's be clear. I'm a realist. I know that the issues I have just named have not been completely resolved; however, progress has been made and that is your role in this world—to help with the progression of humanity. While some people are fortunate enough to see change in their lifetime, you have to realize that you may not and that's OK. Some have lived to see the end of the Holocaust, apartheid,

American slavery, and more. Millions did not either through death or old age and the passing of time. Remember, life is not about the destination. It's about the journey—the journey we are all on together.

You are on a journey. You are part of a journey for change that started long before you were born and if the struggle you are involved in does not change in your lifetime, know that your contributions to the movement are what matter. If you've ever heard me speak about my work to end conflict and genocide in the Congo, you would have heard me say that fighting to end conflict in the Congo is the family business. For literally centuries, my family has been fighting to liberate the Congo from Arab enslavers, Belgian colonialists, and now armed rebel groups who are plundering our country for its natural resources that make their way into our electronics products such as cell phones and laptops. I am fighting hard so that my children will not have to inherit this struggle. If I am not successful, I know that I at least made a dent in the armor of this struggle. In a world with so much uncertainty when I never know when my number may be called, I have to be content knowing that while I was here, I did my best to end the conflict and it will be easier for my children or others to end this conflict.

So relax, relate, and release as Debbie Allen says. It is going to be OK. Do your best and forget the rest like Tony Horton (founder of P90x) says. Your best *is* good enough. All you can do is all you can do so just do it. Lastly, you have to remember that you are living a life that the people you may be fighting to help would literally kill for. Even if you don't live the American high life, just the freedoms you have alone in this country are the envy of many people in different parts of the world. This is not a reason to feel guilty. Live your life because you know it's the life that you want others to live. A life where they don't have to be a slave, or live in abstract poverty; a life where they could go to school without fear of being kidnapped and turned into a child soldier; and a life where you are legally allowed to be treated equally regardless of your gender, race, or religion. This is a reason to celebrate.

So go out and celebrate. Go to the college games. Go to the concerts. Go to the party and drink your apple juice (hey, I can only advocate for so much celebrating). Life is for living. Don't be so caught up in despair that you forget to live the life that you want for those involved in your cause to have. You can change the world and have a good time and it's OK. When I am not out working with upstanders like you, I am spending as much time as possible with my family, playing video games, playing basketball, doing Bikram Yoga, and more. Most importantly, I smile. I wake up every day knowing that we upstanders are closer to victory. The more you work to develop an attitude of success in the movement vs. an attitude of daily despair, the closer to victory you will be!

Activity: answer the following question: what are you fighting to change in the world? What can you do on a daily basis that will keep you the most energized to continue fighting the good fight?

_____

_____

_____

_____

_____

Remember, you owe it to yourself to stay positive and focused on the future. You *will* win if you don't give in!

Chapter 7: G.R.O.W. towards your greatness!

"The moment you become satisfied is the moment you will stop growing."

-Christina Pagliarulo

In my last book *G.R.O.W. Towards Your Greatness! 10 Steps to Living Your Best Life,* I outlined the four key principles that you must live by on a daily basis in order to achieve greatness in everything that you do. The formula works for upstanders especially and so I am tweaking it specifically for you. What does G.R.O.W. stand for? It's simple. Whenever you are encountering a problem that seems to be insurmountable, just remind yourself to G.R.O.W. Make sure you are always focused on G.R.O.W.ing forward and not going backwards. Let's break down the acrostic!

The "**G**" means give. One of the major differentiating characteristics of those who are successful in any business or movement is the quality (not the quantity) of their giving. Earl Nightingale once said that we're all self-made but only the successful will admit it. Many who are not that successful actually walk around with a sense of entitlement and complain about what is owed to them. These people fail to realize that the more they give the more they will receive as opposed to demanding more and receiving less. As I have said before, the more you give, the more you live. Remember, however, you have to give to yourself first, as the creed states. As Iyanla Vanzant said: "Give to yourself until your cup runeth over. Then give to others from the overflow."

Ed Foreman says that you can have everything you want in this life as long as you first help others get what they want. Wayne Dyer says that the more and more you take from the universe; the more and more it is going to take from you. Conversely, the more you give to the universe, the more it will give back to you. Everyone from Oprah to Donald Trump speak to this truth. You may not be able to give $1,000,000 to your favorite organization, your school, or your cause, but you can give the best of whatever skill set you have to your cause. The fact of the matter is, the more you give, the more you get.

The "**R**" stands for release! Let it go, whatever IT is. The strongest example of this is found with the idea of forgiveness. Mark Twain once said that forgiveness is the fragrance that the violet leaves on the heel that has crushed it. One thing that many of us fail to realize is that forgiveness is more important for the person doing the forgiving than the person who is being forgiven. It is you who must release the tension in your body keeping you from advancing. As an upstander, don't spend too much energy hating the perpetrators of atrocities. Forgive them for not knowing what they do and put your energy towards the change you seek to create in this world.

Another important aspect of releasing is letting *them* go. You have to get people out of your life who do not support your cause. Get people away from you who say that you will never stop a war, end poverty, or make education better in your city. Do not let anyone into your life who will implant one seed of doubt in your mind. You are too important to the movement to listen to losers who have no desire to do anything in this world but be average. You're better than average so don't surround yourself with haters. There are enough governments, corporations, and other individuals that already want you to fail. Don't let any more negativity around you!

The "**O**" stands for overcome. Once you release, you have to demonstrate to yourself and others that you have moved on and have become a better person. You have to confront your pain and your fears head on and prove to yourself that your circumstances won't define you, but you will define them. Once you do that, you will be able to define how you will contribute to your movement. Once you do that, you have to overcome the fear that you are going to fail.

Zig Ziglar said that fear is nothing but "**f**alse **e**vidence **a**ppearing **r**eal." The fact of the matter is that more than 80% of what we fear never comes to fruition.

As I said earlier, in the long run, evil always loses out. Genocides end and so does slavery. Forget fear of failure. Overcome the belief that you are not capable to make a dent in the armor of despair. You were built to win!

The "**W**" stands for win. You have to develop a winning mentality. Once you overcome your fear, you must now take that success mindset to every other aspect of your life. If something that you try does not succeed, you have to regroup and try again and keep trying knowing, as Les Brown says, that it's not over until you win.

I used to have a fear of flying. I was like the late Bea Arthur in an episode of *the Golden Girls*. Her character, Dorothy, was afraid of flying but she had to get on a plane with her housemates. When one tried to speak to her, she told her: "Don't look at me when you speak! It'll shake the plane!" That was me 110%! The problem I had was that, as an upstander, I made it my mission to make the world hear my voice and since everyone doesn't have a television around the world (much less cable), I had to figure out how to go to them!

After a great deal of research, I realized it would take too long to boat around the world and speak so flying became my only option. To date, I have traveled to 19 countries and counting. As Dexter Yager said, if the dream is big enough, the problems don't matter. Though I haven't completely conquered my fear of flying (people *can* look at me when they talk to me now), I am confident that I will travel safely to my destination because I am contributing something to humanity so I feel as if I am working for and with the universe.

The winning mentality that helped me conquer my fear of flying has transferred over into everything else I do. I had a fear of starting a business and throwing caution to the wind but I did it because the dream of helping more people and becoming financially secure is not an option for me. I was nervous about getting involved in social justice movements because of what I saw happen to leaders like Dr. King but my dream of seeing global peace and social justice is bigger than my fear of how long I will live (but I *do* plan to be around for a very long time). This winning mentality helped me go from reciting poetry to learning to be a positive rapper, then an actor, and now a motivational speaker. Once I fix my mind on something, it's just a matter of time, in my eyes, before I conquer it because I know it's not over until I win! You have to also know that it's simply not over until we win. We *choose* to upstand. Thus we *will* win. It's as simple as that!

So there it is ladies and gentleman, G.R.O.W.:

> **G**ive
>
> **R**elease
>
> **O**vercome
>
> **W**in!

This formula will work for you in your personal as well as professional life. It will definitely help you as an upstander. If you truly study anyone you admire, you will find that they have utilized this technique in some way, shape, or form. If it worked for them, it can work for you! You have greatness in your future but you have to accept it and prepare for it. No matter what station you find yourself in life, you can indeed G.R.O.W. towards your greatness! Write these steps down in a place that's easy to see! Say it or read it three times a day or more if you need to. Make it happen!

On the next page is a diagram of the G.R.O.W. model. It also appears as a perforated page in the back of this book. Blow it up and put it on your wall if you need to. As you'll see, growing is an iterative process with a singular goal— winning. You may be able to accomplish one of these principles in the circle in a different order than the spelling of the word "G.R.O.W." and that's fine! Just keep G.R.O.W.ing!

G.R.O.W.
Towards Your Greatness

Your winning strategy for personal and professional growth!

The delta or triangle symbol represents change. Once you've developed a winning mentality, you may suffer setbacks that may put you back to one of the other areas on your life raft of success but since you are **focused** on *G.R.O.W.ing* forward you will *never* commit to staying there. The car dealer Sewell said that once you make the commitment to be the best, the majority of your decisions are already made for you because everything you decide to do will be based on being the best! There's no turning back from that!

If this model helps you overcome a family matter, see if you can transfer it over to a problem you may have with a friend. If it is successful there, see if you can apply it to your professional life and then of course, to your cause. Winning a cause simply comes down to who has a stronger will. Work on your will and you *will* win! Anyone or any company that has triumphed has used a similar philosophy. Oprah Winfrey serves as one of the best examples of this principle.

Oprah is very candid about her struggles growing up poor and running with the wrong crowd. When she went to go live with her father, her life started to become more disciplined. As she matured, she found the strength to forgive those who did her wrong. She also forgave herself for some of the things she did not feel proud of. She didn't forget her past, but she released it from weighing her down. The more she began to give (way before the millions), the more society gave back to her. As she overcame her past, she grew stronger and stronger. Now, her winning mentality has transferred from her personal life into the corporate world, to school creation, and beyond! You think this can't work for you as an upstander?

The last exercise is designed for you to seriously start mapping out what you need to do in order to G.R.O.W. towards your greatness. Be seriously thoughtful in how you craft your answers and come back to this often as you continue on your journey as an upstander. The ball is truly in your court. You rhose to be an upstander. Now you must learn how to stand up for yourself. As I said, we will win if we don't give in!

Activity: Time to G.R.O.W.! No more excuses!
What can you do to give back to your community right now?

_____

_____

_____

_____

DO IT!

What do you need to release in order to get on with your life?

_____

_____

_____

_____

LET IT GO!

What obstacles do you need to overcome?

_____

_____

_____

_____

OVERCOME NOW!

What have you been successful in and how can you transfer that success into another area that you are scared to conquer?

_____

_____

_____

_____

_____

WIN!

G.R.O.W.
Towards Your Greatness

Your winning strategy for personal and professional growth!

Other Products From Free Your Mind Publishing

GROW Towards Your Greatness! 10 Steps to Living Your Best Life
Get the motivation you need to live your dreams!
$14.95

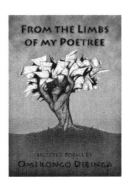

From The Limbs Of My Poetree
Omékongo's first trilingual book of poetry! Available for a limited time with a
special edition, over 90-minute DVD!
$24.95

Poems From The Future: Poetic Reflections From The Next Generation
Read the voices of Westland Middle School's Class of 2005!
$19.95

Pride in my Stride
The first book of children's poetry by Shaumba-Yandje Dibinga
$14.95

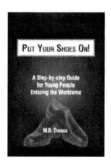

Put Your Shoes On! A Step-by-Step Guide for Youth Entering the Workforce

$14.95

A Young Black Man's Anthem

Omékongo's 1st spoken word CD!
Poetry in English, French, and Swahili!
Winner of the Cambridge Poetry Award for "Best CD"!
$15

G.R.O.W. Towards Your Greatness! Listen to Omékongo's motivational
messages set to music! Introduction by Les Brown!
$9.95

Signs of the Time

Omékongo's 2nd spoken word CD!
Poetry in English, French, and Swahili!

Enhanced CD!
$15

Reality Show
Omékongo's first rap/spoken word hybrid CD
$15

Get your Free Your Mind Publishing T-shirts today in black or white! Baby-tees available in black, white, red, and green!
$15

Front of shirt

Back of shirt

Quick Order Form

Fax orders: (202) 889-5056
Telephone orders: Call (202) 251-7746
Email orders: info@freeyourmindpublishing.com
Postal orders: Free Your Mind Publishing, PO Box 70
Boston, MA 02131, USA

Please send the following books, disks or reports.

_____

_____

Please send more FREE information on:
_ Other Products _ Speaking Engagements _Mailing Lists _Consulting
Name: _____
Address: _____
City: _____ State: ____ Zip: _____
Telephone (day) _____
           (evening) _____
Email: _____
__ Please add me to your e-mail mailing list!

Sales tax: Add 7.75% sales tax for products shipped to California addresses.

Shipping by air
U.S. $5.50 for first book, $4.50 for CD and shirts, and $2.50 for each additional product.
International: $9.00 for first book or disk; $5.00 for each additional product (estimate)

Payment: _Visa _MasterCard _Optima _AMEX _Discover
Card number: _____
Name on card: _____ Exp. Date: _____

"Opening eyes, one mind at a time."

FREE YOUR MIND
P U B L I S H I N G